RHYTHM GAMES
for perception & cognition
by Robert M. Abramson

revised edition

AF173993

CONTENTS

Editor: DEBBIE CAVALIER

Typesetting: SHARON HARRIS, MAEGONIA RICH

Cover Design: JORGE PAREDES

Layout: THAIS YANES

 ONLINE ACCESS INCLUDED

 To access audio visit:
alfred.com/redeem

Enter this unique code:

00V017CD-69445608

♩♫ INTRODUCTION

Throughout history, women, men, and children have enjoyed playing rhythmic games for the pleasure derived from total physical movement and mental concentration focused on successful activity. For this reason, all of the exercises in this book on musical rhythm are cast in the form of movement games.

Here are some of the values to be gained from using the games in this book:

1. Children need games in order to grow and develop skills of attention, concentration, cooperation, social integration, clarity of expression, and the ability to notice and express the slightest variation in nuance (shading) of sounds, movements and feelings in order to react with clarity of expression.

2. Rhythmic Games have been used to teach numbers, letters, formulas, progressions and rules of order and behavior which need to be remembered even when children are excited.

3. Rhythmic Games develop objectivity. The players in a Rhythmic Game can observe their own behavior and decide if and when corrective changes are needed. They know if their activity is skillful or not skillful and can measure their own growth. This results in increased and realistic self esteem as practice produces skill. By allowing and encouraging self-correction, the leader reduces authoritarian behavior or external approval.

4. Rhythmic Games develop small and large muscle groups and a sense of balance by forcing the use of both sides of the body independently and in exercises of coordination and disordination. These games also allow for skillful and conscious practice of swinging, throwing, catching, walking, running, galloping, skipping, and hopping.

5. Rhythmic Games teach teamwork as well as flexibility of response to the changing demands of the game.

6. Rhythmic Games lead players to notice different degrees of skill in different players and develop a respect for individuality.

7. Rhythmic Games highlight growth as a process towards mastery. When players first play the games they are challenged to realize that skills need to be developed.

8. Rhythmic Games cannot be memorized so they are always new and never boring.

The games in this book are based on the methods and principles of the Swiss educator Emile Jaques-Dalcroze. They are designed to help students of all ages develop rapid and accurate connections between the EARS that listen, the BRAIN that analyzes, and the BODY that acts to interpret the messages encoded in the music. As in all Dalcroze based work, the music does the teaching and the teacher (or leader) simply acts as a model and a coach.

Though musical game activities have many forms, only three are introduced in this volume:

1. The QUICK REACTION invites the players to listen for musical signals that signify a rapid change in activity.

2. The FOLLOW asks the player for infinite variation in nuance during an activity to match changes in music of tempo, energy, accent, and pauses. It develops flexibility and creative responses.

3. The INTERRUPTED CANON asks the players to remember a new sequence of activities while they are still performing a previous activity. It requires independence of expression and the ability to be in two time zones simultaneously: the present and the future.

TEACHER'S NOTE:

The basic progression in these movement and music games is from movement in place to the more difficult movement in space: from movement of hands, fingers, arms, shoulders and torso to movement of legs and feet. Games using balls, sticks, and bean bags are used in the early games to avoid self consciousness about body movement in front of other people. As students become more skillful with rhythmic speech and body movements (clapping, swinging) to complete locomotion (walking, jogging), verbal commands ("GO, STOP, CHANGE, BACK") must be given loudly and clearly at least one or more beats before the command is to be performed. The common words can be made easier if the leader adds the word AND before the command word is given. Commands of change should not be given until the players have had a chance to experience the original activity for a minimum of 16 to 32 beats.

It is especially helpful in slow tempo games for the students and leader to speak the instructions for movement while the games are being played. Special care must be taken to pronounce the words for the entire length of the beat.

Do not be surprised if these games and the music provided on the accompanying recordings provoke opportunities for laughter and other slightly noisy expressions of joy in learning!

Audio icons throughout the book indicate the corresponding track number on the recording.

♪ PRELUDE TO CHAPTER I

Before playing the games of Chapter I, it is important to practice the skills of movement for the hands, wrists, forearms, full arms, shoulders and torso necessary for using the body as a rhythmic instrument. It is also useful to practice moving the head and neck and eyes from left to right, right to left, as well as up and down, so that players are free to follow the movements of the ball from themselves to their partners or teammates. This will help develop the social and cooperation skills used in skillful play.

Before using real balls in the first games in Chapter I, it is useful to use balls made from crinkled paper. Crinkled paper balls will not roll away when dropped and can be fashioned to fit into the smallest of hands.

1. Roll a crinkled piece of 8" x 10" paper or newsprint into a ball.

2. Pass out one ball to each student.

3. Facing the students, the teacher can model various ways of passing the ball from hand to hand, swinging overhead several times, from front to back of the body and so on. Next the teacher can touch the ball to a body part (nose, head, chest, shoulder, knee) before passing the ball to the other hand. Be sure to use a very moderate and regular tempo. The teacher should also set a verbal rhythm such as, "AND PASS, AND PASS." This verbal chant should emphasize the "AND" word because that is the true rhythmic moment rather than the moment that the ball is placed in the next hand. The students can follow these movements and should be encouraged to chant the words "AND PASS" with the teacher.

4. Have the students (using the paper ball) create a variety of activities: swinging the arms to the front, to the back, over the head, between the legs. During these activities the teacher and students can chant the words "AND PASS" at a very moderate tempo. Next, repeat the activities at a moderately fast tempo, and then repeat the same movements at a slow tempo. Vary the space between the hands (more space for slow and less space for fast tempos) to make the movements easier.

5. Have the students pass the ball from their right to their left hand and then back to their right hand without throwing or dropping the ball. Stop the activity and ask the students to hold the ball in their left hand and pass to the right. It is important that the students learn to place the ball gently but firmly in the palm of the receiving hand. Practice wrist rotation, bringing the palms up and palms down with the hands in preparation for passing the ball around a circle of students.

During these activities remind the students to keep their hands ready and their eyes on the ball. As a final test, have them pass the ball with their eyes closed to increase their sense of space, touch, direction, velocity and balance. Practice at a moderate tempo with moderate space. Later, add new and more difficult movement time and space combinations such as fast tempo with large arm space; wide arms with slow tempo; close arms with slow tempo and so on. The variations are infinite.

Give each player a chance to be the leader and to invent new ways of passing the ball.

Social Integration and Cooperation Skills:

Playing PASSING THE SQUARE

1. A student faces the teacher and they play PASSING THE SQUARE with a paper ball while the other students watch, count and then mime the activity. Be sure to count "AND" between each number.

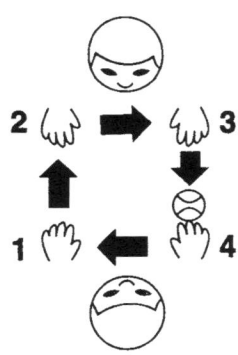

When this is performed successfully, start the game in the opposite direction (counter-clockwise).

2. The teacher performs this in duet with different students.

3. All students form duet teams with one ball per team and practice the same game following the ball with their eyes (eye-hand coordination).

4. Finally, all students stand in a circle. The teacher demonstrates the two-handed pass in a clockwise direction. Each student has two beats to receive the ball with both hands and then turn and pass the ball to the next student with both hands. They must follow the ball with their head, neck and eyes.

5. Have the students try the game in a counter-clockwise direction allowing the right and left hemispheres of the brain to get equal play.

As soon as the students have learned to hold and pass the ball securely in any tempo, all of these exercises can be repeated with real balls and other passable items such as tennis balls, beach balls or nerf balls. Items such as bean bags, wooden blocks and even a pencil or a stick will allow new sensations of weight and balance and teach new skills to enlarge the students' vocabulary of movement.

♪ CHAPTER I - TEMPO GAMES

Tempo is the term used to indicate the basic rate of speed of musical movement - i.e., slow, moderate, fast, becoming faster, becoming slower.

♪ Game No. I PASSING THE BALL - Moderate Tempo

PURPOSE:
To develop skill in ensemble, listening, and poise in starting and stopping a rhythmic activity; to develop spatial judgment in relation to other people; to coordinate hands, fingers, and wrists.

EQUIPMENT: One tennis ball, one drum.

FORMATION: Students sitting in a circle.

DIRECTIONS:
The teacher demonstrates how the ball is to be passed from student to student in a clockwise direction on each beat of a moderate tempo. The teacher then sets and maintains the tempo (walking speed) on the drum. At the teacher's verbal command "GO" the students begin the game. At the command "STOP" the students and the teacher stop all activity. It is helpful for the students to speak the word "PASS" in rhythm while they play this game.

EXAMPLE:

Variation No. I
The students listen to the teacher's drum beat. At the verbal command "GO" they begin the ball-passing game. When the teacher stops playing, the students stop the game as quickly as possible. When the teacher begins to play again, the students resume the game.

Variation No. 2

The students listen to the teacher's drum beat. At the verbal command "GO" they begin the ball-passing game. At the teacher's command "CHANGE" the students change the direction of the ball-passing activity. At first, the teacher's command to "CHANGE" should be given infrequently. As the students become more skillful, the command to "CHANGE" can be given more frequently in order to challenge the students to quicker reactions. When the teacher stops playing, the students should stop the game as quickly as possible.

Track 3

Variation No. 3

The same as Variation No. 2, but the command "CHANGE" is now indicated by playing a sound on the rim of the drum. The students must now respond to the verbal signal "GO," the musical signal "STOP" (indicated by stopping the drumming), and the command "CHANGE" (indicated by a different quality of sound from the drum).

TEACHER'S NOTE:

Each of these games should also be played in standing and kneeling positions. In addition to passing the ball, rolling or bouncing it from student to student can be used for more challenging variations.

Game No. 2 PASSING THE BALL - Fast Tempo

Track 4

PURPOSE: To discover the space and energy relationship necessary for smooth and efficient performances at a fast tempo.

EQUIPMENT: One tennis ball, one drum.

FORMATION: Students sitting in a circle.

DIRECTIONS:

The teacher sets and maintains a running tempo on the drum. At the verbal command "GO" the students pass the ball around the circle on each beat in a predetermined direction. When the teacher stops playing, the students stop the game as quickly as possible. When the teacher begins to play again, the students resume the game.

TEACHER'S NOTE:

At first this will be difficult. A smooth performance can be encouraged by having the students sit very close to each other, as there is a reciprocal effect between fast movement and small distance. Try having the students change from a sitting to a kneeling position in the circle. This will free the torso and make turning and passing easier.

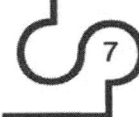

♩♪ Game No. 3 PASSING THE BALL - Slow Tempo

PURPOSE: To develop perceptive and cognitive efficiency of movement in a slow tempo.

EQUIPMENT: One tennis ball, one drum.

FORMATION: Students sitting in a circle.

DIRECTIONS:
The teacher sets and maintains a slow tempo. At the verbal command "GO" the students pass the ball around the circle on each beat in a predetermined direction. When the teacher stops playing, the students stop the game. When the teacher begins to play again, the students resume the game.

Variations
Try Game No. 3 using the variations previously mentioned: students standing or kneeling in a circle; rolling or bouncing the ball to one another; using the command "CHANGE" to indicate a change of direction in passing the ball.

TEACHER'S NOTE:
Demonstrate and urge the students to use a slow, smooth movement of the entire arm when passing the ball to one another in order to feel the full length of the beat. Encourage the students to discover that more space between them makes the movement more poised.

Game No. 4 PASSING THE BALL - Accelerando (Getting faster);
Ritardando (Getting Slower)

Track 7

PURPOSE: To develop skill and flexibility in changing speeds and in relating these time changes to energy, space, and movement efficiency.

EQUIPMENT: One tennis ball, one drum.

FORMATION: Students sitting on the floor in a circle.

DIRECTIONS:
The teacher establishes a moderate walking tempo on the drum. At the verbal command "GO" the students begin to pass the ball around the circle on each beat in a predetermined direction. Now the teacher varies his tempo at random, getting faster or slower. The students must follow the tempo changes. When the teacher stops playing, the students stop the game as quickly as possible.

EXAMPLE:

Variation No. I Bouncing
Game No. 4 can be played on a more advanced level by bouncing or rolling the ball from student to student, or by introducing one additional ball moving in the same direction. When two balls are used, the students must look in both directions and be prepared to pass very quickly. These game variations may also be played in two concentric circles, one circle passing a ball clockwise, the other passing it counter-clockwise.

Track 8

Variation No. 2 Rolling

Track 9

● = Students
✳ = BALL

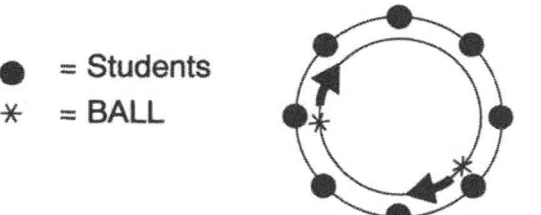
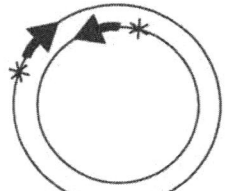

TEACHER'S NOTE:
The teacher must encourage the students to change their spatial arrangement for efficiency (closer for fast tempi, further apart for slow tempi).

♪ Game No. 5 BOUNCE AND CATCH

PURPOSE: To judge tempo outside of one's own body space.

EQUIPMENT: One tennis ball, one drum.

FORMATION: One student stands in the center of a circle of standing students.

DIRECTIONS:
The teacher demonstrates that the student in the center is to bounce the ball to one student in the circle. The receiver catches the ball on the second beat and bounces it back to the center on the third beat. The center player catches on the fourth beat. The game continues in this manner, going around the circle. The teacher sets and maintains a moderate tempo on the drum. At the verbal command "GO" the students begin the game. Bounces and catches must be on the beat. When the teacher stops playing, the students should stop the game as quickly as possible.

TEACHER'S NOTE:
All of these games relate time, space, and energy as concepts basic to efficient movement and realization of tempo. It is helpful for the students to speak the tempo as they play this game: "BOUNCE-CATCH; BOUNCE-CATCH."

♪ Game No. 6 CATCHING THE BALL

PURPOSE: To develop individual use of time, space and energy for tempo recognition and realization.

EQUIPMENT: One tennis ball for each student, one drum.

FORMATION: Students standing, scattered freely throughout the room.

DIRECTIONS:
The teacher demonstrates throwing the ball up on the first beat and catching it exactly on the second beat. The teacher sets and maintains a moderate tempo on the drum. At the verbal command "GO" the students begin to throw and catch the ball. When the teacher stops playing, the students should stop all activity and freeze in position.

EXAMPLE:

Game No. 7 CLAPPING THE BEAT

PURPOSE: To use clapping as the physical realization of a perceived tempo.

EQUIPMENT: Piano, drum, voice, or percussion instruments.

FORMATION: Any.

DIRECTIONS:
The teacher sets a tempo by clapping the beat. At the verbal command "GO" the students clap the same tempo the teacher has set. As soon as the teacher stops, all students must stop immediately. This game should also be played with the students closing their eyes so that the signal is purely aural.

Variation
One student is chosen as conductor and chooses a tempo to clap. As soon as possible, the other students join in realizing the tempo. The teacher then chooses another student to find a different speed. Students should be encouraged to try a variety of tempi, from very, very fast to extremely slow.

TEACHER'S NOTE:
A variety of clapping movements can be used for this game: clapping the tips of the fingers, the tips of the fingers into the palm of the other hand, palms together, or cupping the hands to capture air and make a loud popping sound. Care must be taken to keep the wrists flexible, and to use as much space between the hands as necessary to feel the full length of the beat in slow tempi.

Game No. 8 SWINGING THE BEAT

PURPOSE: To use more of the body in the perception and realization of tempo.

EQUIPMENT: Piano, drum, voice, or percussion instruments.

FORMATION: Students scattered throughout the room, an arm's distance apart.

DIRECTIONS:
The students explore various ways of swinging the arms, keeping the torso and knees free and loose. Swings of different sizes and different directions can be used. One student is chosen as conductor and is asked to demonstrate arm swings at any speed he chooses. The other students imitate the movement.

When the conductor-student stops, the students freeze their positions. Now the teacher sets a new tempo — on a drum, piano, or by speaking the words: "SWING, SWING, SWING." At the verbal command "GO" the students try to find the size of swing which will fit comfortably with the tempo the teacher has set. This game should be played in all tempi.

🎼 Game No. 9 ORCHESTRATING THE BODY

PURPOSE:
To help the student discover the many possible uses of the hands, wrists, forearms, elbows, upper arms, and torso, in making efficient movement to fit a wide variety of tempo situations.

EQUIPMENT: Piano, drum, voice, or any other instrument.

FORMATION: Students scattered throughout the room, standing at least an arm's distance apart.

DIRECTIONS:
The teacher demonstrates and helps the students to explore tiny swings made with the fingers, slightly larger swings made from the wrist, slightly larger swings made from the forearm, larger swings made with the whole arm, and very large swings made with the arm and the torso, with the knees bending freely. Swings should be performed with both arms, experimenting with parallel and contrary motion and moving from side to side and/or front to back. The teacher sets a regular tempo on drum, piano or by speaking the word: "SWING." The students try to find the most efficient movement for the tempo the teacher is playing. The game begins at the verbal command "GO" and ends when the teacher stops playing or speaking the beat.

EXAMPLE:

Variation
The teacher varies the tempo at random, using accelerando (getting faster) and ritardando (getting slower). The students try to respond quickly and accurately to the changes of speed, using whichever part of the body (fingers, hands, wrists, arms, forearms, or the entire body) will most effectively realize the tempo of the moment.

Game No. 10 WALKING THE BEAT

PURPOSE: To use movement in space to perceive and realize tempo and ensemble; to become aware that moving the body in space creates shifts in weight and balance.

EQUIPMENT: Drum, piano, or voice.

FORMATION: Students standing in a circle, ready to move in a predetermined direction.

DIRECTIONS:
The teacher should prepare the students by demonstrating a good starting position: all the weight on the front leg, the front knee slightly flexed, the back leg ready to move at the command "GO." This position can be experienced more deeply by having the students bounce on the knee of the forward leg. When the students are in the ready position, the teacher sets and maintains a moderate tempo on the drum, piano, or with the voice, speaking the word "WALK." At the verbal command "GO" the students begin to march around the circle, taking one step for each beat. As soon as the drum, piano or voice stops, the students must stop in a position of complete poise.

EXAMPLE:

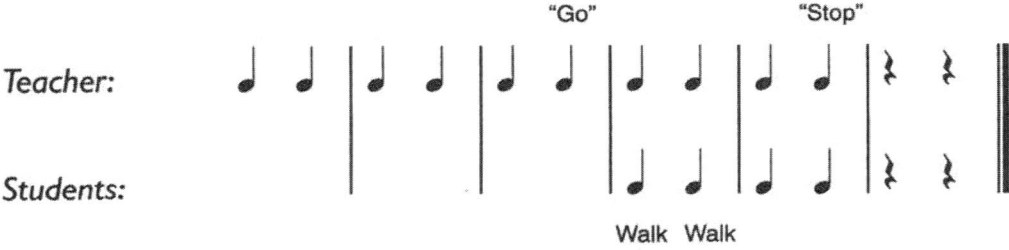

TEACHER'S NOTE:
At first the students will have difficulty in stopping as soon as the instrument signaling the beat stops. Some will fall forward, some will fall backward, some will bounce up and down on one leg. In order to be successful and efficient at this game, it is very important to develop a sense of upright balance. This can be done in several practice runs, in which the students are suddenly instructed to stop with the body held very tall on a very straight spine. Any leaning forward or backward will tilt the student off balance and make his position unstable.

Variation No. 1
The same game at running tempo.

TEACHER'S NOTE:
It is much more difficult to stop the forward motion with precision, poise, and balance at a fast tempo. It is important to make the running tempo exactly twice as fast as the walking tempo.

Variation No. 2

Track 17

The teacher should demonstrate a variety of smooth, long, sliding steps at a slow tempo (twice as slow as a moderate walking tempo), speaking the word "SLOOOOW" for the entire duration of each step. Both feet should remain on the floor. The teacher sets and maintains a slow tempo on the drum, piano, or by repeatedly speaking the word "SLOOOOW." Starting from a ready position (one leg advanced, knee slightly flexed, with all the weight on the front leg), the students are to walk the teacher's beat taking large sliding steps in order to feel the full length of the beat. The game begins at the verbal command "GO." As soon as the drum, piano, or voice stops, the students should stop in a position of complete poise.

Variation No. 3

Track 18

Taking long, sliding steps (both feet should remain on the floor), and walking at slow, elephant-walk tempo (twice as slow as a moderate walking tempo), the students move around the circle in a predetermined direction, simultaneously clapping their hands. There should be one step and one clap on each beat. Both the space between steps and the space between the hands should be large enough to experience the full length of the beat.

Game No. II WHICH PART MOVES?

Track 19

PURPOSE: To develop quick reactions and skill in the coordination and dissociation of the hands and feet.

EQUIPMENT: Drum, piano, or voice.

FORMATION: Students standing in a circle in a good starting position, ready to move in a predetermined direction.

DIRECTIONS:

The teacher sets and maintains a walking tempo on the drum or piano, or by repeatedly speaking the word "WALK." At the verbal command "GO" the students begin to march and clap simultaneously, one step and one clap on each beat. At the verbal command "CHANGE" the students stop the forward marching movement but continue to clap on each beat. At the next command "CHANGE" the students begin to march and clap simultaneously. When the music stops the students freeze in a position of poise.

Variation

Track 20

The game begins with the students standing in place in a circle, facing a predetermined direction. At the verbal command "GO" the students begin clapping the beat that the teacher has established. At the verbal command "CHANGE" the students stop the clapping and begin walking, one step on each beat. At the next command "CHANGE" the students stop marching and resume clapping while standing in place.

TEACHER'S NOTE:

This game and variation should be played at walking tempo, running tempo, and at the slow, elephant-walk tempo.

Game No. I2 SKIPPING OR GALLOPING THE BEAT

PURPOSE: To use two new movements to realize a tempo.

EQUIPMENT: Piano or drum.

FORMATION: Students standing in a circle, facing in a predetermined direction, in a good starting position.

DIRECTIONS:
The teacher plays a skipping or galloping rhythm on the drum or piano. The students are instructed to skip or gallop the beat which the teacher sets. At the verbal command "GO" the students move around the circle, taking one skip or gallop on each beat. When the music stops, the students freeze in a position of poise.

Skipping

TEACHER'S NOTE:
At a moderate tempo the skip or gallop is very easy. At a slow tempo the students must skip or gallop higher into the air in order to feel the full length of the beat. At a fast tempo the skip or gallop hardly moves into the air at all.

EXAMPLE:

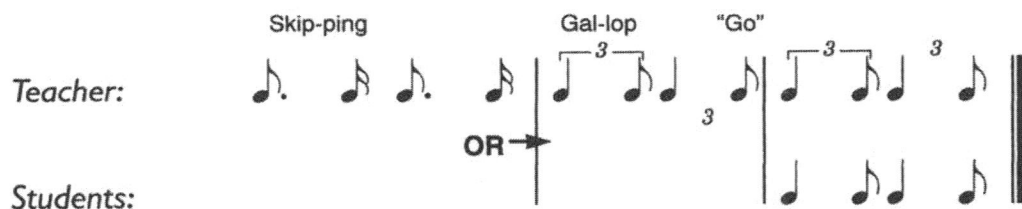

 # Game No. I3 COUNTING TO EIGHT

PURPOSE: To develop the students' memory for beat and tempo.

EQUIPMENT: Piano or drum and one tennis ball.

FORMATION: Students sitting in a circle.

DIRECTIONS:
The teacher demonstrates that he will play and count eight beats at a regular tempo. As soon as he has finished counting and playing the eight beats, the students pass the ball around the circle for eight beats in the same tempo, and stop. Now the teacher plays eight beats, counting out loud, in a new tempo. After the eighth beat, the students immediately respond by passing the ball at the new speed for eight beats, arranging their space for speed and efficiency. Practice this game until the students are proficient at it in all tempi.

♪ CHAPTER II - DYNAMICS GAMES

Dynamics refers to the various energy levels of music, movement, or speech. In music these levels are indicated by the following signs:

pp - Pianissimo   = Very Soft
p - Piano   = Soft
mf - Mezzo Forte   = Moderately loud
f - Forte   = Loud
ff - Fortissimo   = Very Loud
Crescendo   = Gradually getting louder
Diminuendo   = Gradually getting softer

In movement games louder dynamic levels can be realized by using more space, more of the body, and/or more energy. Less space, less of the body, and/or less energy is used to express softer dynamic levels.

TEACHER'S NOTE:

It is best to begin games of dynamics at a moderate rate of speed. As the students become more proficient, the teacher can introduce different tempi (ranging from very fast to extremely slow) as well as diminuendo and accelerando.

♪ Game No. I SWINGING (Loud, medium, soft)

Track 24

EQUIPMENT: Drum or piano.

FORMATION: Students standing an arm's distance apart, scattered throughout the room.

DIRECTIONS:
The teacher should help the students experiment with various ways of swinging their arms and with various sizes of arm swings. The teacher sets and maintains a moderate tempo on the drum or piano, at a moderate dynamic level. At the verbal command "GO" the students try to match the dynamic level of the teacher's playing by swinging their arms from side to side to each beat of the music. When the music stops, the students stop all activity.

Variation

Track 25

The teacher sets a regular tempo but varies the dynamic level of his playing. The students attempt to match the size and energy of their arm swings to the level of dynamics played by the teacher. When the teacher plays loudly (forte), the students should take bigger swings, using more of the body. When the teacher plays softly (piano), the students should take small, light swings using little space and very small movements.

Game No. 2 TREES IN THE WIND

Track 26

PURPOSE: To realize dynamic changes with proper orchestration of body parts.

EQUIPMENT: Piano, drum, or voice.

FORMATION: Have the students form an interesting forest of tree shapes, using fingers for leaves, forearms and upper arms for branches, and legs and torso for the trunk of the tree.

DIRECTIONS:
The teacher demonstrates and helps the students to discover various ways of expressing dynamic intensity: fingers can move very quietly, expressing a pianissmo (very soft) level. Various combinations of other body parts, such as wrist motion, forearms, upper arms, torso, legs, knees, and the entire body can express greater dynamic intensity. After this exploration, the teacher plays, speaks, or sings at various dynamic levels. Pretending to be trees in the wind, the students attempt to realize quickly and efficiently the changes of dynamic level by using different parts of the body. When the music stops, the students should freeze their position.

 # Game No. 3 PAWS ON THE FLOOR

Track 27

PURPOSE: To develop the muscles of the fingers, wrists, arms and body in response to changes in dynamics.

EQUIPMENT: Drum, piano, or voice.

FORMATION: Students sitting on the floor.

DIRECTIONS:
The teacher helps the students explore the use of fingertips, wrists, and easy arm motion, using the floor as a drum. First use the hands as if they were the paws of a small animal, expressing softness by light, quick, darting movements (piano) with a fast rebound from the floor (piano). Then press the palms of the hands and the fingers more heavily against the floor (mezzo forte). Finally, add the forearms and upper arms, always rebounding quickly from the floor (forte). The teacher begins to play or speak at a moderate tempo and at a moderate dynamic level. At the verbal command "GO" the students try to express as accurately as possible any changes in dynamic level which the teacher makes, using the hands in parallel motion and drawing upon the vocabulary of movements practiced above.

Variation No. I
Beginning with the right hand, the students try to express as accurately as possible the dynamic level which they hear the teacher play. At the verbal command "CHANGE" the students continue the game using the left hand.

Track 28

Variation No. 2
Students play the game using the hands alternately or together, depending on the teacher's verbal commands: "LEFT HAND," "RIGHT HAND," "BOTH HANDS."

♪ Game No. 4 THE FIVE STEPS

PURPOSE: To coordinate the use of space, time, and energy in realizing various dynamic levels. To control and coordinate the large muscles of the legs and the small muscles of the feet and ankles.

EQUIPMENT: Drum or piano.

FORMATION: Students standing in a circle in a ready position (all the weight on the front foot, with the front knee slightly flexed), facing in a predetermined direction.

DIRECTIONS:

The teacher demonstrates and the students imitate various sizes of steps. Step No. 1: a tiny walking step on half-toe; Step No. 2: about the size of one's own foot; Step No. 3: a regular walking step; Step No. 4: a little larger; Step No. 5: a leap. The game begins with the teacher playing pianissimo (very softly) at a moderate tempo on the drum or piano. At the verbal command "GO" the students begin to move around the circle, using Step No. 1 on each beat. When the teacher calls out "STEP NUMBER TWO" and changes the level of playing to piano (soft), the students change to Step No. 2. When the teacher changes to mezzo forte (medium loud) and gives the command "STEP NUMBER THREE," the students change to Step No. 3. When the teacher changes to forte (loud) and gives the command "STEP NUMBER FOUR," the students should change to Step No. 4. When the teacher changes to fortissimo (very loud) and gives the command "STEP NUMBER FIVE," the students should change to Step No. 5. When the music stops, the students freeze their position.

Variation

The teacher calls out any number from one to five at random, adjusting the dynamic level of his playing to correspond. The students respond with the proper size steps. The teacher's tempo should remain constant.

TEACHER'S NOTE:

It is very important that the commands for the sizes of the steps, and the loudness or softness of the music be coordinated.

Game No. 5 THE FIVE CLAPS

PURPOSE: To coordinate hands and arms in space in order to realize varying degrees of dynamics from very soft (*pp*) to very loud (*ff*).

EQUIPMENT: Drum, piano, or voice.

FORMATION: Students sitting in a circle or scattered freely throughout the room.

DIRECTIONS:
The teacher demonstrates and the students imitate various ways of clapping, using more and more space between the hands and arms to indicate a greater dynamic level. There should be five sizes of claps, corresponding to the five steps already explored: These should range in size from No. 1 (very small), indicating pianissimo, to No. 5 (very large), indicating fortissimo. The game begins with the teacher playing pianissimo (very softly) at a moderate tempo on the drum or piano. At the verbal command "GO" the students begin to clap the beat, using clap No. 1. When the teacher calls out "CLAP NUMBER TWO" and changes the dynamic level of his playing to piano (soft), the students change to clap No. 2. When the teacher changes to mezzo forte (medium loud) and gives the command "CLAP NUMBER THREE," the students change to clap No. 3. When the teacher changes to forte (loud) and gives the command "CLAP NUMBER FOUR," the students change to clap No. 4. When the teacher changes to fortissimo (very loud) and gives the command "CLAP NUMBER FIVE," the students respond with clap No. 5. When the music stops, the students stop all activity.

Game No. 6 THE FIVE STEPS AND THE FIVE CLAPS

PURPOSE: To develop coordination between the upper and lower body through a combination of stepping and clapping games.

EQUIPMENT: Drum or piano.

FORMATION: All students standing in a ready position in a circle, facing in a predetermined direction.

DIRECTIONS:
Beginning at mezzo forte (medium loud), the teacher sets and maintains a marching tempo on the drum or piano. At the verbal command "GO" the students step and clap simultaneously each beat of the music, using step and clap No. 3. When the teacher calls a number from one to five (changing the dynamic level of his playing accordingly), the students immediately change the size of their steps and claps to correspond to the command. When the music stops, the students stop all activity.

Variation No. 1

Without verbal commands, the students respond to changes in the dynamics of the teacher's playing. In this game the students begin to use their own judgment about size of steps and claps.

Variation No. 2 THE DIMINUENDO (gradually getting softer)

Using fortissimo drumbeats, the teacher sets and maintains a moderate marching tempo. At the verbal command "GO," the students begin moving around the circle, using step and clap No. 5. When the teacher changes the dynamic level of his playing to forte and gives the command "NUMBER FOUR," the students change the size of their steps and claps to correspond. When the teacher changes to mezzo forte and gives the command "NUMBER THREE," the students again change the size of their steps and claps. When the teacher changes to piano and gives the command "NUMBER TWO," the students change to step and clap No. 2. When the teacher changes to pianissimo and gives the command "NUMBER ONE," the students change to step and clap No. 1.

Track 31

Variation No. 3

The same as Variation 2, except the teacher omits the verbal commands. Students respond to changes in the dynamics of the teacher's playing.

Variation No. 4 THE CRESCENDO (Gradually getting louder)

The same as Variation 2, except the teacher and students begin at the pianissimo level and progress at a regular tempo to the fortissimo level.

Track 32

Variation No. 5

As the students become more proficient at realizing the crescendo, the teacher can omit the verbal commands. Students must immediately respond to changes in the dynamic level of the teacher's playing.

Variation No. 6

One student is chosen as conductor and stands in the center of the circle. The student conductor uses gestures to show the size and dynamic level of the five steps and the five claps. The rest of the students and the teacher, playing the drum or piano, try to realize the dynamic levels indicated as quickly as possible.

Game No. 7 SWINGING THE CIRCLE

Track 33

PURPOSE: To develop a sense of ensemble; to feel the unity of dynamics in a group.

EQUIPMENT: Piano or drum.

FORMATION: Students standing in a very large circle, holding hands, arms stretched open.

DIRECTIONS:
The teacher joins the students in the circle and demonstrates how to pull from left to right, shifting body weight from leg to leg in a swinging movement. The students practice pulling from side to side, using a minimum of space and movement at first and increasing their activity until they are leaping in the air. The game begins when the teacher sets and maintains a moderate tempo for swinging on the drum or piano. At the verbal command "GO" the students begin to pull and swing in rhythm from left to right. As the teacher changes the dynamic level of playing, the students respond with stronger pulls (corresponding to the dynamic levels forte and fortissimo) or weaker pulls (corresponding to the dynamic levels piano and pianissimo). Students stop as soon as the music stops, and freeze in position until the teacher gives the verbal command "REST."

♪ Game No. 8 MEETING THE LINE

PURPOSE: To discover the relationship between time (speed), space (duration), and energy (dynamics).

EQUIPMENT: Piano and drum and a marker (masking tape, chalk line, bean bags, or large sheets of paper) to mark the center of the room and starting positions.

FORMATION: Two groups of students, one at each end of the room, standing shoulder to shoulder and facing the center of the room.

DIRECTIONS:
Markers should be placed so that the students can see the center of the room and starting positions. The teacher sets and maintains a moderate tempo on the drum or piano, and indicates the number of steps the students are to use to reach the center of the room. At the verbal command "GO" the students must try to reach the center line in exactly that number of steps, taking one step on each beat. When the teacher completes the command number of beats he stops playing, and the students must freeze in their positions. The teacher again sets a tempo on the drum or piano and indicates the number of steps to be used for returning to place. At the verbal command "GO" the students are to walk backwards to their starting positions, using the given number of steps and looking over their shoulders so they can see where they are going. When the teacher completes the command number of beats he stops playing, and the students must freeze in position.

TEACHER'S NOTE:
It is imperative that the students reach their destination in exactly the number of steps called for, taking one step on each beat and keeping the lines very straight. The number of command steps will determine the quality of the movement. If the students are to use only three steps to reach the center, they will have to leap on each beat. If the students are to use only three steps to reach the center, they will have to leap on each beat. If the command number is thirty, they will have to take very small steps.

CHAPTER III - ACCENT GAMES

Accent is a sudden release of energy on any beat or on any part of a rhythmic pattern. In some cases the musical sign > under a notehead indicates an accent.

Track 34

Game No. I STATUES

PURPOSE: To distinguish between and respond quickly to accented and unaccented beats; to exercise inhibition of the will.

EQUIPMENT: Drum or piano.

FORMATION: Students sitting, standing, or lying on the floor with enough space to move their bodies.

DESCRIPTION:
After playing several unaccented beats in a moderate tempo on the drum or piano, the teacher suddenly inserts a loud, heavily accented beat, simultaneously calling out the word "ACCENT." The students are instructed to make a new statue each time they hear an accented beat and the verbal command "ACCENT." They should freeze in the position of the statue until the next accented beat and command. At first, the accented beats and commands should come at regular intervals. When the students are familiar with the game, the teacher should omit the verbal command and play the accents at irregular intervals. As proficiency increases, any student who moves on an unaccented beat is declared "out." The game continues until one player is declared the winner.

EXAMPLE:

Game No. 2 ROUND AND STRAIGHT

PURPOSE: To realize quickly and accurately accented and unaccented beats; to exercise inhibition of the will.

EQUIPMENT: Drum, piano, or voice.

FORMATION: Students lying on the floor, scattered throughout the room.

DIRECTIONS:
The teacher demonstrates how to curl the body in to a small round ball. He then demonstrates a long, straight body position on the floor. The students should imitate both positions. The teacher decides which shape (round or straight) will begin the game, and all students assume that shape. The teacher plays or speaks unaccented beats in a moderate tempo. Students are instructed to change body shape and freeze the movement only when they hear a sudden loud "ACCENT" being played.

EXAMPLE:

Variation No. 1
After sufficiently practicing Game No. 2, any student who moves or changes body shape on an unaccented beat, or who chooses the wrong body shape, is eliminated from the game. The game continues until one player is declared the winner.

TEACHER'S NOTE:
The easiest version of this game requires many unaccented beats between accented beats. To make the game more challenging, play the accented beats more frequently and at irregular intervals, until the changes are on each beat with silences between beats.

Variation No. 2

Students in a squatting position, with their arms on their knees or overhead as the teacher directs. All students assume the starting position, changing only when they hear an "ACCENT" being played.

EXAMPLE:

Variation No. 3

Have the students express the "ACCENT" using various parts of the body — e.g., knees, elbows, hands, shoulders, torso, feet, etc. — and various combinations of body parts.

 Game No. 3 CHANGE DIRECTION

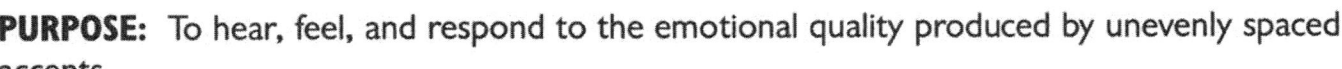

Track 36

PURPOSE: To hear, feel, and respond to the emotional quality produced by unevenly spaced accents.

EQUIPMENT: Drum, piano, or voice.

FORMATION: Students standing, scattered throughout the room.

DIRECTIONS:

The teacher demonstrates marching to a beat in one direction. At the teacher's verbal cue "ACCENT" he demonstrates a sharp and sudden change of direction to the left, to the right, or backwards. The game begins with the students in a good starting position, all the weight on the front foot. The teacher plays, speaks, or sings unaccented beats in a marching tempo. At the teacher's command "GO" the students begin to march forward, taking one step on each beat. When the teacher plays or speaks an accent, the students quickly change direction as the teacher demonstrated.

They continue to march on the beat in the new direction until the next accented beat. When the music stops, the students quickly change direction as the teacher demonstrated. They continue to march on the beat in the new direction until the next accented beat. When the music stops, the students stop all activity.

Game No. 4 JUMP THE PUDDLE

PURPOSE: To develop quick reactions to accented beats, using horizontal and vertical space.

EQUIPMENT: Drum, piano, or voice.

FORMATION: Students standing in a circle ready to move in a predetermined direction.

DIRECTIONS:
The teacher and students should explore various ways and directions of jumping on one and both feet. The teacher demonstrates how slightly flexed knees will allow for a gentle rebound. When the students have explored jumping forwards, backwards, sideways and turning in the air, the game begins. The students decide on one type of jump. The teacher plays, speaks, or sings unaccented beats in a moderate tempo. At the command "GO" the students begin to move around the circle, taking one step on each beat. When the teacher plays an accented beat, the students react quickly by pretending to jump over a puddle of water. If accented beats occur in succession, the students jump on each accent. When the teacher resumes playing unaccented beats, the students return to their marching steps. When the music stops, the students freeze their positions.

EXAMPLE:

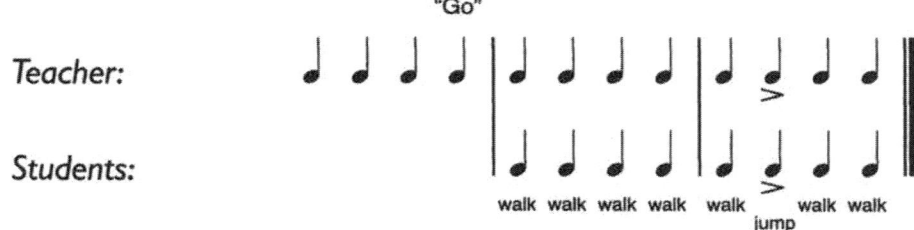

Game No. 5 JUMP AND TURN

PURPOSE: A more challenging version of games one through four.

EQUIPMENT: Voice, piano, or drum.

FORMATION: Students standing in a circle, ready to move in a predetermined direction.

DIRECTIONS:
The teacher plays, speaks, or sings unaccented beats in a moderate tempo. At the verbal command "GO" the students begin to move around the circle, taking one step on each beat. When the teacher plays an accented beat, the students jump and turn in the air, and resume marching on the beat in the new direction. When the music stops, the students freeze their positions.

EXAMPLE:

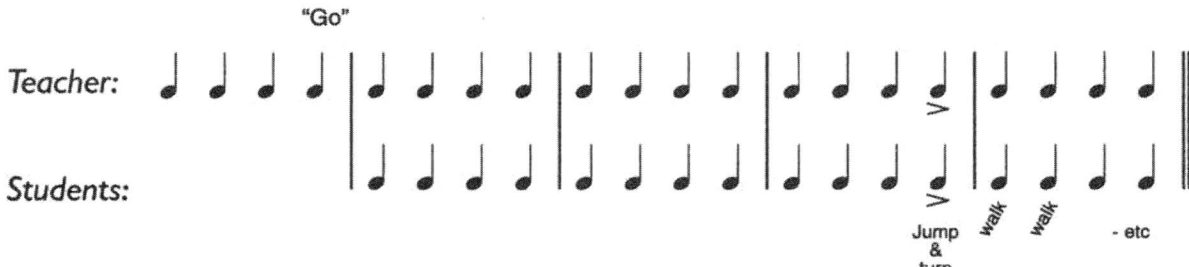

Variation
The same game can easily be played with a song, poem, or rhyme. The teacher sets a tempo on the drum. At the verbal command "GO" the students begin walking to the teacher's beat, singing a song or speaking a rhyme. When the teacher's voice and drum produce a sudden "ACCENT," the students jump and turn in the air, and resume marching to the song or rhyme in the new direction.

EXAMPLE:

♪ Game No. 6 WORDS AND CHANGES

PURPOSE: To explore the potential of accent in language.

EQUIPMENT: None.

FORMATION: Students sitting in a group.

DIRECTIONS:
The teacher demonstrates the difference between speaking a sentence with and without accents.

EXAMPLE:
Teacher: MA-ry had a little lamb
The students reproduce the same sentence with an accent on a different word or syllable.

EXAMPLE:
Student: Mary HAD a little lamb!
Or: Mary had a LIT-tle lamb!

Variation
Play this game with a variety of sentences.

Game No. 7 PUNCHING THE BAG

Track 39

PURPOSE: To realize accents using the hands, arms, wrists, shoulders, and torso.

EQUIPMENT: Drum, piano, or voice.

FORMATION: Students standing, scattered throughout the room, ready to imitate a boxer punching a punching bag.

DIRECTIONS:
The teacher demonstrates the difference between regular, unaccented punches and sudden, sharp, accented punches. The students imitate both movements. The teacher plays unaccented beats in a regular tempo (moderate, slow, or fast) on the drum or piano, or with the voice. At the verbal command "GO" the students begin to punch the bag, using regular, steady movements, one to each beat. When the teacher plays an accented beat, the students direct a sudden release of energy at the "punching bag." The game continues with the teacher alternating unaccented and accented beats at random. When the teacher stops playing, the students stop all activity.

Variation No. I
The same game can be played imitating the movements of hammering. Gentle taps of the hammer equal regular, unaccented beats. On accented beats the students respond with a sudden release of energy on the hammer stroke, followed by a large rebound.

Track 40

TEACHER'S NOTE:
This game should be played with both the left and right hands in order to develop bilateral symmetry.

Variation No. 2   RINGING THE BELLS
The teacher demonstrates and the students imitate the movements of pulling up and down on a bell-cord. The teacher plays unaccented beats in a slow tempo on the drum or piano, or with the voice. At the verbal command "GO" the students begin to "pull the bell-cord" up and down, using one pull on each beat. When the teacher plays an accented beat, the students respond with a quick, sudden, short pull downward, and a slow release.

Track 41

🎵 CHAPTER IV - GAMES OF RESTS

A rest is a period of active, measured silence. In movement a rest means an immediate cessation of activity while remaining poised. In music, rests are used to replace sound for the purposes of pattern, phrasing, articulation, and contrast. Most rests are carefully measured. In musical notation the following signs are used to replace sounds of specific duration:

EXAMPLE:

Sounds	*Rests*
o	▬
𝅗𝅥	▬
♩	𝄼
♪	𝄿
♪.	𝄿·

Game No. 1 CAN YOU STOP? — CAN YOU START?
(Moderate Tempo)

PURPOSE: To develop coordination, quick response, and a feeling for the precise measurement of silence.

EQUIPMENT: Drum or piano.

FORMATION: Students sitting.

DIRECTIONS:
The teacher sets and maintains a moderate tempo on the drum or piano. At the verbal command "GO" the students clap the tempo which the teacher has set. When the teacher calls any number from one to ten, the students must clap silently for that number of beats while they count the number out loud in rhythm. They then resume regular clapping until the next number is called.

EXAMPLE:

Variation No. 1   CAN YOU STOP? — CAN YOU START? (Slow Tempo)
The teacher sets and maintains a slow tempo on the drum or piano. At the verbal command "GO" the students clap the tempo which the teacher has set. When the teacher calls a number from one to ten, the students must mime clapping for that number of beats, counting the number out loud in rhythm. They then resume regular clapping until the next number is called.

Variation No. 2
The same game played at a fast tempo.

TEACHER'S NOTE:
Slow tempi are difficult. Breathing in rhythm (inhaling on one slow beat and exhaling on the next) helps to keep the tempo steady. If counting is done out loud during the silent beats, the numbers must be spoken slowly and evenly for the entire length of the beat.

Game No. 2 THE DISAPPEARING BEATS

PURPOSE: To control movement, measure silence, and remember a sequence of events.

EQUIPMENT: Drum or piano.

FORMATION: Students sitting.

DIRECTIONS:
The teacher demonstrates eight even beats (moderate tempo) by clapping his hands and counting out loud, carefully accenting the first clap. At the verbal command "GO" the students imitate clapping and counting the eight beats in the tempo established by the teacher. The teacher now demonstrates counting and clapping seven beats, but mimes and whispers the eighth beat.

EXAMPLE:

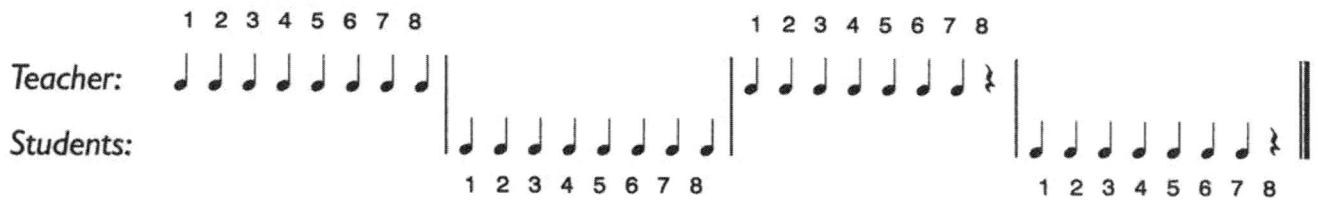

The students imitate the teacher's pattern. The teacher then demonstrates and the students imitate six claps, followed by two silent mimed claps to total eight.

EXAMPLE:

The teacher next demonstrates, and students imitate, the following combinations:
Five claps, followed by three silent mimed claps to total eight.
Then: four claps and four silences mimed and whispered.
Then: Three claps and five silences mimed and whispered.
Then: Two claps and six silences mimed and whispered.
Then: One clap and seven silences mimed and whispered.
Then: All eight beats silent, followed by a shout or stamp of the foot to signify the end of the series.

The students now follow the teacher through the entire series. Now the game begins. The teacher establishes a moderate tempo on the drum or piano. At the verbal command "GO" the students attempt the entire series of audible and mimed claps, while the teacher plays the series on the drum.

TEACHER'S NOTE:
Maintain a steady tempo throughout the sequence.

Track 46

Variation No. 1
Perform the series by clapping the hands on the notes and snapping the fingers on the silences.

Variation No. 2
The teacher sets a moderate tempo on the drum or piano. At the verbal command "GO" the teacher stops playing and the students perform the entire series. The teacher plays only the first beat of each group of eight.

Track 47

Variation No. 3
Students standing in a circle facing a predetermined direction. At the verbal command "GO" the students move around the circle, taking one step on each audible beat. Do not step on the silences.

Track 48

 # Game No. 3 THE MYSTERIOUS REAPPEARANCE
OF THE MISSING BEATS

PURPOSE: To control movement, measure silence, and remember a sequence of events.

EQUIPMENT: Drum or piano.

FORMATION: Students sitting.

DIRECTIONS:
The teacher demonstrates eight silent mimed claps (moderate tempo).
Then: seven mimed claps and one audible clap.
Then: six silent claps and two audible claps.
Then: five mimed claps and three audible claps until the sequence reaches eight audible claps.
The teacher plays a regular tempo on the drum. At the verbal command "GO" the students try to reproduce the entire sequence, clapping and counting the audible beats and miming and whispering the silent beats, while the teacher plays the sequence on the drum.

Variation No. 1
Combine Games 2 and 3 as illustrated by the following:

TEACHER'S NOTE:
Capitalized numbers are vocalized; lower-case numbers are mimed and whispered.

"ONE-TWO-THREE-FOUR-FIVE-SIX-SEVEN-EIGHT"
"ONE-TWO-THREE-FOUR-FIVE-SIX-SEVEN-eight"
"ONE-TWO-THREE-FOUR-FIVE-SIX-seven-eight"
"ONE-TWO-THREE-FOUR-FIVE-six-seven-eight"
etc., until all eight beats are mimed and whispered.

"one-two-three-four-five-six-seven-EIGHT"
"one-two-three-four-five-six-SEVEN-EIGHT"
"one-two-three-four-five-SIX-SEVEN-EIGHT"
"one-two-three-four-FIVE-SIX-SEVEN-EIGHT"
etc., continuing the series until the class reaches:
ONE-TWO-THREE-FOUR-FIVE-SIX-SEVEN-EIGHT
clapped and spoken.

Game No. 4 FILL IT IN

PURPOSE: To recognize and analyze the measurement of silence.

EQUIPMENT: Drum or voice.

FORMATION: Students sitting.

DIRECTIONS: The teacher plays or speaks a rhythmic pattern which includes rests.

EXAMPLE:

or

The students listen to the pattern and try to determine by counting quickly where and how much silence is used. They then fill in the missing beats with clapping.

Variation
As they become more familiar with the game, individual students can be chosen to create new patterns with rests. The other students must fill in the rests with movements, clapping and/or counting.

EXAMPLE:

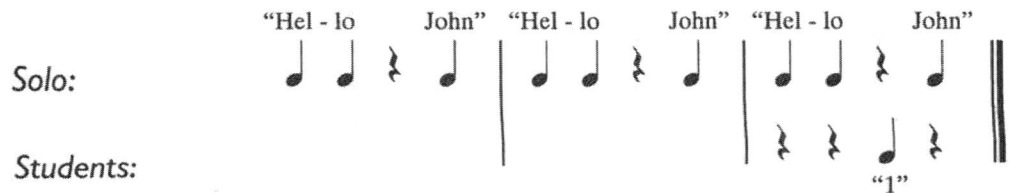

♩♪ Acknowledgments

The author would like to acknowledge, with appreciation, the following people whose contributions, real and symbolic, made these workbooks possible:

EMILE JAQUES-DALCROZE, innovator of Eurhythmics, whose revolutionary ideas in music and movement are yet to be fully explored.

HILDA M. SCHUSTER, Director of the Dalcroze School of Music, New York City, my first teacher in Eurhythmics, who introduced me to the joy and excitement of the world of rhythm.

CARL L. LEEDS, for his constant support and helpful advice above and beyond the bonds of friendship, and all of my close colleagues in the United States, Europe, and Asia.

Last but not least, my thanks to the thousands of students, of all ages, who have helped me to understand music and movement as a humanizing life-force.

Robert M. Abramson

Theory Department
Manhattan School of Music
New York City

Prof. Of Music
The Juilliard School

Co-Director
The Dalcroze School